Understanding

Anger

During

Bereavement

Bob Baugher, Ph.D.,

TABLE OF CONTENTS

First Printing .... May, 2000
Second Printing .... January, 2003
Third Printing...........July, 2008

Introduction

Grief is like a tapestry of many colors. Your tapestry has its own, unique design. Tapestries of grief get their color from the subtle shades of: emptiness, loneliness, numbness, fear, anxiety, hurt, guilt, impatience, bitterness, sadness, discouragement, apathy, helplessness, and hopelessness. Woven throughout these tapestries of grief is the bright red thread of anger. Used carelessly, the threads of anger can tear apart the fabric of your soul. Guided by this booklet, you may be able to begin to untangle the jumbled threads of grief and use the threads of anger creatively to bind your tapestry together into a comforting quilt.

It is not unusual to experience feelings of anger following the death of a loved one. Yet, you don't have to be angry to be bereaved. Some people go through intense bereavement without experiencing anger. Other people experience anger as one of several grief reactions. And still others experience anger as raw, gut-wrenching, and ever-present. The painful feelings associated with your grief may be difficult to understand. Even more confusing are the feelings of anger that you, or those around you, are experiencing. When anger is turned inward, it may be experienced as depression, guilt, and/or lowered self-esteem. In some cases, turning anger inward may lead to suicidal thoughts and behaviors. Anger turned outward, however, can communicate important information. It can also hurt others.

This booklet will help you learn more about yourself and people close to you. We are not going to tell you not to be angry. One of the most important messages you will see throughout this booklet is: **It's okay to be angry; but you must choose what you will *do* with your anger.** Some choices have helpful results; others result in hurtful behavior. Just as it is up to others to gain further insight into and work on their hurtful anger, only you can determine when you are ready to do the same. If you are ready, let's explore anger by first looking at how it has been described by experts and then how it has affected your life. From there we will explore factors that contribute to anger, how anger is expressed, targets of anger, and finally, suggestions for coping with it.

1

WHAT IS ANGER?

Compare these descriptions:

Webster's New World Dictionary defined anger as:
> A feeling of displeasure resulting from injury, mistreatment, opposition, usually showing itself in a desire to fight back at the supposed cause of this feeling. [1]

Therese Rando, Ph.D., stated that:
> Anger is always to be expected to some degree following a significant loss. It is a natural consequence of being deprived of something valued. [2]

Anger is described in the book <u>Prescription for Anger</u> as
> ... a normal, natural emotion that, in itself, is neither good nor bad. Instead its value is determined by how you choose to respond to it. It is up to you to decide whether anger will be a negative or positive emotion in your life. [3]

Michael Lewis, from Robert Wood Johnson Medical School noted,
> True anger is an evolutionarily useful trait that helped us overcome obstacles. Behind socially destructive actions is "rage" —which is directed broadly, not at a specific problem. Unlike true anger, rage is fueled by a need to repair a damaged self-esteem. [4]

Neal Clark Warren, Ph.D., author of <u>Make Anger Your Ally</u>
> stated Anger is an impressive gift which comes as part of our biological inheritance. Anger is a physical state of readiness . . . . We are highly alert. So when we are angry, all the power of our person is available to us. This, and this alone, is anger. Preparedness. Power. It can be brought under our cognitive control, and when it is, we become far more effective in the way we cope with life. It equips us to act decisively in the interest of resolution and healing. [5]

ANGER INSIGHT SURVEY

What are your anger reactions? Using the following survey, respond according to how you are feeling at this moment. Your answers could vary from day to day. It may be difficult to sort out which of your angry feelings are related to loss and which are due to other factors. Don't worry about that now. As you continue through this booklet, you'll become more skilled at identifying the sources of your anger.

1. When I get angry, I _____ my anger is related to the death of my loved one.
   a. am immediately aware if
   b. gradually become aware if
   c. am not usually aware if
   d. am never really sure if

2. Words I'm most likely to say to others when I'm angry are:
   _____
   _____

3. Words I'm most likely to say to myself when I'm angry at myself are: _____
   _____

4. When I get angry, the amount of control I **usually** feel over my anger is:
   a. None   d. Some   f. Almost total control
   b. Almost none   e. Quite a bit   g. Complete control
   c. A little

5. When I get angry, it is at a specific event or person (rather than at the world in general).
   a. Never   c. Some of the time   e. Always
   b. Once in a while   d. Quite often

6. The person I most often get angry with is: _____
   and it is usually because: _____

7. When I get angry, it happens very quickly.
a. Never	c. Once in a while	e. Quite often
b. Seldom	d. Some of the time	f. Always

8. It takes _____ to get me angry.
a. almost nothing	e. quite a bit
b. very little	f. a great deal
c. a mild irritation	g. a tremendous amount
d. a moderate irritation	

9. When I get angry, it usually lasts for
a. just a few seconds & it's over	h. several hours
b. quite a few seconds	i. the remainder of the day
c. a minute or two	j. into the next day
d. several mintes	k. several days
e. 15-30 minutes	l. one to four weeks
f. 1/2 hour to two hours	m. a few months
g. a few hours	n. several months or more

10. Circle each of following statements with which you agree or strongly agree
    a. I hurt deep down beyond any words.
    b. Sometimes I feel like I'm going to blow up.
    c. There is a person I can't forgive for hurting me like this.
    d. I feel a part of me has been cut from my life.
    e. I am angry for all the pain I'm going through.
    f. It feels like I will never love (or be loved) again.
    g. Anger is the major feeling I have during the course of a day.
    h. Anger seems to be controlling my life.
    i. I hate life.

Before you move to the next page, please answer the following:
   1. What have I learned about myself so far? Can I put it into words?
   2. What, if any, changes do I wish to make?

Later in this booklet you will be asked to fill out another survey that will help you focus on the reasons for your anger, on your anger-related feelings, and your targets of anger.

What Causes Anger?

Anger can be triggered by one event or a combination of reasons. Some of the most common reasons are:

Frustration	Stolen future
Learned helplessness	The manner of death
Imbalance	Self-blame
Revenge	Low self-esteem
Ego defense mechanisms	Thinking errors
Failure to receive expected support	Reinforcement

Frustration

Everyone has goals to accomplish with the important people in their life--parents expect to see their children grow and become adults, spouses and partners look forward to spending their lives together, siblings assume that their brothers and sisters will be around, children may expect their parents to live a long life, and friends and lovers have plans to go places and do things together. Some bereaved people report feeling abandoned. The death of your loved one has likely left you with many unfulfilled goals. What are they? When your goals are blocked, you may feel frustrated at the blockage. Intense frustration *can* escalate into anger.

Learned Helplessness

The death of someone you love can leave you feeling overwhelmed by negative thoughts, feelings, or situations. When people feel hopeless because they cannot control painful events, they may gradually develop a sense of helplessness. When people don't know how to control the pain in their life and feel they have reached the end of their rope, they feel they have nothing to lose. They may unleash their anger at themselves or others by hurting themselves, attempting suicide, or lashing out at others. If you are experiencing these destructive feelings, which are not unusual following a tragic death, do not act on them. To repeat, despite what you may be feeling, <u>do not hurt yourself or others</u>. Find a counselor, therapist, or someone who can help you.

Imbalance

Life is a balancing act. Throughout life we strive to find the balance between things such as work and pleasure, hunger and fullness, wakefulness and restfulness, and playfulness and seriousness. The death of an important person in your life has likely thrown your life completely out of balance. As time passes, you may feel "Nothing is the same—nothing will ever be the same." You may be angry at what the death has done to your family members. You may now view life with a different set of priorities as you realize that you don't have the patience you once had. As you gather your diminished energy to try to hold the remaining pieces of your life together, you're faced with the challenge of finding a new center of balance. When your anger is aroused after you have been knocked off balance, it is often targeted at people who appear insensitive to the significant disruptions you are facing in your life.

Revenge

You may feel victimized and revengeful after the death of your loved one. These feelings are strongest when the death was a homicide, suicide, or the result of someone's irresponsible behavior. If you are considering acting on your feelings, ask yourself, "What if I hurt someone, how much more grief would this put on my loved ones? (See page 12 for help on redirecting feelings of revenge.)

Ego Defense Mechanisms

It is natural to seek immediate remedies for damages to one's sense of self (ego), or to one's emotions. Temporary remedies for these situations are called "defense mechanisms." *Cancellation, denial, displacement, projection, and rationalization* are the most frequently used defense mechanisms in response to anger.

Cancellation is an attempt to erase the harmful impact of your angry behavior. Apologizing, repenting, and asking for forgiveness are all efforts to wipe the slate clean and start over.

Yet the cycle repeats. People using this defense may insist that they are not in need of assistance, yet their good intentions are not sufficient to halt their abusive anger.

Denial involves ignoring your intentions or not accepting personal responsibility for controlling your anger. For example, a few weeks following the death of her ten year-old son in an auto accident, a mother denied that she yelled and screamed at the children who were making noise in front of her house. She stated, "Sure my voice was a little loud, but I didn't yell and scream."

Displacement, sometimes called *Scapegoating*, is the process where you actually shift your anger away from the individual or situation that was originally aggravating to you. Instead of yelling at the person who caused the accident, the mother in the previous example may have been displacing her anger onto the children.

Projection is the process of attributing one's own feelings or shortcomings to someone else. People who yell at others for being rude may actually need to reduce their own rudeness. We may use projection when we find it too threatening to recognize our own hurtful behavior.

Rationalization involves attempting to find rational justification for one's own irrational behavior. An example of rationalization would be the woman who screams and swears at another customer who took 12 items in a nine-items-or-less checkout line, then attempts to justify her angry outburst by adamantly pointing to the check stand sign, saying, "Read the sign and count his items. Am I right or not?" Rationalization is also frequently used to justify one's self-destructive behavior.

Failure to Receive Desired Support

The death of your loved one may have left you feeling alone in your grief. Caring people in your life can, at times, lighten some of the negative feelings. The following actions taken by supportive people are often appreciated by those who are grieving:
1. Talking about the person who died
2. Permitting crying
3. Listening without judging
4. Offering to help and then following through

5. Permitting the bereaved person to grieve at his or her own pace, without imposing time limits
6. Calling and saying, "I'm here."

When you fail to receive such gestures of support, or when the people around you believe they are helping when actually they are not, anger often fills the void, together with disappointment, sadness, and intensified feelings of loneliness. These feelings are often aroused when others tell you what you *should* (or should not) be feeling.

Stolen Future

The death of someone we love means that our future with that person has been taken away. This is one reason that the death of a young person is so difficult for many people. We expect a child to be in our life as we watch him or her grow, play, laugh, continue in school, graduate, and become an adult. However, even with an older person, we still may expect to spend many more years with this person. When a 79 year-old woman's obituary appears in the newspaper, people who read it and don't know her may say, "At least she lived a full life." This is little consolation to her husband, children, and grandchildren. They had looked forward to many more years with her. We all know that the future is promised to no one. But when it has been taken away by an unexpected death, you may feel cheated. And for some, the reaction is anger.

The Manner of Death

Any cause of death has the potential to bring out angry feelings. Heart disease, cancer, stroke, liver failure, AIDS, alcoholism, to name a few, may trigger angry feelings in the survivors. Anger is often directed at multiple targets when death results from homicide, suicide, accidents, or unknown causes. In these situations, anger is aimed at the perpetrator, other parties involved, and the justice system including the police, judges, policies, procedures, and laws. A related source of anger is lack of accountability--the failure of a person or agency to admit partial or full responsibility for the death. In addition, anger may be directed at the person who died, the physician and other hospital staff, the mental health system, even newspaper and television reporters.

Self-Blame

When people blame themselves for the death of a loved one, they often compound their grief with feelings of guilt, remorse, depression, shame, and/or anger. Have you blamed yourself in some way? If so, how? The difficulty with self-blame is that it doesn't matter whether you had any actual responsibility for the death. The critical feature is that you *perceive* you are partially or fully to blame for the death. It is difficult to talk people out of such a belief. Other reasons for self-blame are:

1. Not having spent enough time with the person
2. Not having spent enough quality time
3. Not living up to expectations
4. Not grieving "right," e.g., too angry or not angry enough

If you have been blaming yourself, we have a question for you:

What would it take to forgive yourself?

Low Self-Esteem

A loved one's death can affect how we feel about ourselves. Bereaved people typically experience lower self-esteem following the death. They may say some of the following statements to themselves: "I don't know who I am anymore." "I don't like living this way." "I feel lousy." Because people with low self-esteem may be more likely to have a lower threshold for anger, bereaved people may also have lower than normal anger thresholds. Have you found yourself or the people around you getting more upset at life in general? As people work through their bereavement, both their self-esteem and threshold for anger may begin to rise.

Thinking Errors

Rigid patterns of thinking are related to anger and lowered self-esteem. Sometimes thinking occurs so rapidly or subtly that it seems impossible to answer the question "What are you thinking? At other times, thinking is similar to an internal conversation. This is called "self-talk." Rigid patterns of self-talk arise from assuming that our own needs should take priority over anyone else's. Three characteristics common to the thinking errors listed below are self-centeredness, irresponsible behavior, and nonempathic feelings.

Let's look at two commonly used thinking errors [6]:

Closed Channel is a thinking style in which a person disdainfully ignores or rejects the opinions of others, yet insists their own opinions are listened to and respected. Their self-talk of *Closed Channel* is, "my opinion is the only one that counts." This may be manifested in a bereaved person expressing anger at others for the way they are (or are not) grieving. The message of the grieving person using closed channel is, "Everyone's expressions of grief should look just like mine."

Uniqueness is shown in the person who adheres to the mistaken notion of specialness. People using *Uniqueness* believe that rules which apply to others do not apply to them. The message of the grieving person using uniqueness is, "I'm the only one who has a right to be angry about this death."

A reaction that can increase the use of Thinking Errors is called **Emotional Detachment.** When bereaved people respond to the death of their loved one by becoming emotionally detached, their thinking is generally dominated by angry self- or other-directed statements which reflect their unrealistic expectations of themselves and others. The Thinking Errors **Blaming** and **Excuse-making** are frequently used by individuals who are emotionally detached.

They often blame others for their anger and quickly create excuses for their angry behavior. The message of these individuals is, "It is my right not only to get angry, but to *stay* angry."

Reinforcement

Some anger-based behaviors are repeated because they have been reinforced in the past. Yelling at someone may give us an immediate sense of power, especially if it gives us what we want. Immediate reinforcement may be the reason some people fall into the pattern of self-punishment. For example, a man whose son died in a car accident responds by hitting his fist into the palm of his other hand. He discovers that this action reduces his focus on the horrendous pain of his grief. Over time, the bereaved father's fist-hitting continued because of the immediate reinforcement he received from the hitting action. Later we will discuss how your responses to your angry feelings can become a habit.

What Is Positive About Anger?

Anger Can Effect Positive Changes in Society

When the energy from anger can be channelled into a positive outcome, the benefits can be significant. The countless examples include:
> laws have been changed
> key issues have received new or renewed respect and attention
> support groups have been formed
> safety standards have been strengthened
> products have been improved

Anger Can Communicate Our Dissatisfaction with Another Person's Behavior

The past few pages described some of the typical causes of grief-related anger. Many of the causes (frustration, revenge, failure to receive desired support, the manner of death) involve other people. The death of someone you love can motivate you to speak out to other people in ways that can bring positive changes. For example, one of the reasons that Erin Linn [7] wrote her book, <u>I Know Just How You Feel. . . Avoiding the Cliches of Grief,</u> was because of her angry reaction to the unhelpful advice people gave in their misguided attempts to help bereaved people. How can you use your anger in a positive way to possibly bring about a positive change in another person?

Anger Can Change in a Positive Way How We Interact with Other People in Our Life

We know that anger can cause problems when it's out of control. The more control we have over our anger, the more we can control the way we treat others. For example, anger at yourself for failing to tell the person who died how you feel can motivate you to express yourself with the important people in your life. To whom in your life do you need to express how you feel?

11

WHAT IS NEGATIVE ABOUT ANGER?

Anger Can Incite More Anger

"Anger begets anger" is a common saying about anger. For many people, once they begin the process of acting out their anger, those actions produce even more intense feelings of anger. This ever-accelerating anger cycle is all too common. For example, it can begin with a man, justly angry about something, slamming his fist on the table. Rather than relieving his anger, the fist-slamming energizes him to yell and slam even more. His face gets redder, and his muscles tighten until the fist-slamming escalates into chair-throwing.

Anger Can Hurt Others

For most of us, the worst aspect of anger is when we hurt other people. Since most anger outbursts occur in the home, the people we hurt are often the ones we care about the most. With whom were you last angry? Do you wish you could express your anger in less hurtful ways? If you're not sure, or you answered "yes," keep reading.

Anger Can Focus on Revenge

Some people have thoughts such as:
"I'll get even with him . . . He's not going to get away with this . . . She's going to suffer like I have . . . They're going to regret this . . . This isn't fair—he's going to get what's coming to him . . . I'll give them something they'll never forget."

People seeking revenge think and plan what they might do if they came into contact with the person responsible for the death of their loved one. They may have detailed fantasies of the scenarios they would like to see happen. In the news there are daily reminders of immoral, illegal, incompetent, and unjust situations and our anger may be so intense that we scheme some action to "right" the wrong inflicted on some other innocent victim.

Feelings of revenge are common, especially when someone's actions have deprived us of a loved one. If you are having feelings of revenge, answer the following:

"Are these feelings disrupting my life-style?"

"Am I so focussed on getting revenge that I am neglecting someone or something else in my life?"

"Has this aspect of my anger and grief interfered with my other relationships or my ability to complete my activities of daily living?"

If the answer to any of these questions is "yes," or "probably," then you might benefit from counseling or finding a friend who can listen to you discuss how to refocus your anger into positive action. Mothers Against Drunk Driving (MADD) is an example of bereaved people working together to channel their angry and revengeful feelings into helping others.

Anger Can Make Things Worse when it:

Hurts others

Makes us look bad

Cuts communication

Scares people away from us—temporarily or permanently

Damages material goods

Prevents us from receiving feedback from others about our behavior.

Anger Can "Leak Out"

If you are not aware of your intentions, your anger might be leaking out in subtle ways. Examples are: snide comments, picking on another person (going beyond good-natured teasing), looking for a fight, exaggerating the extent of another person's mistakes, and generally seeing the negative in everything.

Question: How can you become aware of your intentions?

Answer: *Listen to your self-talk.*

Or ask a good friend to give you feedback.

13

A positive example of using self-talk to clarify one's intentions is demonstrated by a father who is angry at his 17 year-old daughter and wants to convey his message without "losing it." He says to himself, "I hope I confront her in such a way that she'll be able to sense how much love and respect I have for her. I want her to know that I'm angry with her and that it is not my intention to hurt her." This type of self-talk can be hard to do, but the benefits are endless. We'll discuss this further, beginning on page 41 in the section on *"I" messages*.

Anger Can Lead to Passive and Passive-Aggressive Behavior

People who express their anger in passive-aggressive ways are sometimes unaware of their own hidden intentions, or they don't always notice how their passive-aggressive expressions of anger are subtly eroding their relationships, until those relationships crumble. Passive-aggressive expressions of anger are hurtful in indirect ways and are often used by people who want to manipulate others. They are also used by people who want to express their anger, hurt, or frustration without receiving the repercussions associated with more direct expressions of anger.

Direct, aggressive expressions of anger are designed primarily to attack and eliminate resistance to the angry person's goals. The indirect, *passive-aggressive* and purely *passive* expressions of anger are typically used when the angry person wants to resist the other person. Examples of each form of anger expression are:

Direct--shouting, verbal or physical attacks

Indirect (which involves passive-aggressive behaviors) --being unavailable, pouting, or sulking

Purely passive--procrastinating or "conveniently forgetting" to do something you had promised to do

It is often difficult for the recipient of passive or passive-aggressive expressions of anger to "prove" that those expressions were intended to be hurtful. The truth is, the hurt caused by passive and passive-aggressive anger is just as painful and destructive as the more obvious and measurable damage caused by aggressive expressions of anger.

Anger Can Deflect Other Emotions

Because anger is such a powerful emotion, it can consume a bereaved person's focus for a time after a death. When anger's intensity begins to fade, various other grief reactions come into view. For example, a woman's husband died as a direct result of unsafe conditions at the factory where he worked. She was furious and sued the company. Two years later, when the trial ended, her feelings of vindication were short-lived because she began experiencing a flood of awaiting grief reactions, including depression, guilt, fear, and loneliness. Learning more about the role anger plays in your life can help improve your ability to cope with other emotions.

Anger Can Harm Your Health

The scientific research on anger is clear: Anger can lead to heart attack. People who have frequent outbursts of anger or those who show high levels of hostility when they become angry have higher risks for heart attack.

Anger Can Put You Out of Control

If you have ever gotten out of control with your anger, think of the last time that happened and answer the following questions:

What were the circumstances?
What did you say?
What behaviors did you exhibit?
Were you or others in danger at any time?
How did the other person respond?
What emotions were you feeling at the time?
How did you feel immediately afterwards?
How did you feel later on that day or the next day?
What kind of physical harm does anger do to your body?
What are you feeling now as you review your behavior?
How do you think the other person feels about your actions?

Reading this booklet and making a commitment to reduce the likelihood of losing control in the future is an important step.

Disorders and Problems That Can Contribute to Anger and Other Emotional Outcomes During Bereavement

There are a number of factors that can put bereaved people more at risk for anger problems. None of these factors are to be considered excuses for permitting anger to become out of control. The first three on the list are conditions that may need referral to a therapist. Suggestions for coping with anger will be discussed beginning on page 38.

Mood and Anxiety Disorder

People who are coping with depression, bipolar disorder (manic-depression), or anxiety disorders may be more irritable and experience a lower tolerance to handle daily frustrations.

Head Injury

A person who has been knocked unconscious for more than several minutes and later reports problems with short-term memory, concentration, and depression may also have frequent anger control problems. This may also be true for people who have had a period of unconsciousness due to toxic fumes (e.g., carbon monoxide poisoning) or a stroke.

Borderline Personality Disorder

People with Borderline Personality Disorder show instability in relationships, mood, and self-image. Their attitudes and feelings toward other people may change rapidly and inexplicably. They may be argumentative, irritable, sarcastic, quick to take offense, and in the heat of their emotional flurry, they may self-mutilate. Although little research has been done on how these individuals handle their grief, it seems likely that their preexisting emotional problems, including anger, would be amplified. Only trained therapists are able to help these individuals.

Nutrition and Eating Problems

The death of a loved one can alter one's food intake. Many bereaved people lose interest in food, while some use food in excess as a source of comfort. Energy loss during bereavement can take the motivation out of going to the grocery store, preparing the food, and eating it. It is common for bereaved persons to have nutritional deficiencies. Some of these deficiencies are known to affect mood, including irritability and anger.

Sleep Problems

Sleep disruptions are a common accompaniment to depression and bereavement. Research on REM (rapid eye movement) deprivation indicates that, during the day following a night of REM-disrupted sleep, people show higher levels of irritability. Seeking help with sleep disruptions can be an especially important step toward anger control.

Substance Use

When alcohol is used as a way to cope with the pain of grief, one of the effects is the decrease in inhibitions. We have all seen the effect that alcohol can have on someone who is already angry. If your alcohol use has contributed to the display of angry feelings toward a person in your life, ask yourself, "What can I do about this?" and find a way to reduce or eliminate your alcohol use. If you cannot, can you ask someone for help? The same can be said for ingestion of other drugs, including stimulants or barbiturates.

Pre-Existing Emotional Styles

Another approach toward understanding individual differences in anger reactions is to explore various styles of thinking and feeling. The following descriptions are presented only as guidelines to help you gain insight into your own anger reactions and of those around you. They are presented in terms of their extremes, which may oversimplify how individuals may cope with anger. Much research is needed in order to determine how these emotional styles fit together into a composite picture. In addition, because there is a variety of predisposing tendencies that influence anger arousal, the "one size fits all" method of anger control does not work. You'll find a broad selection of approaches to anger control in the last section of this booklet.

Feelers vs. Thinkers

"Thinking-oriented" people evaluate problems and situations more logically than "feeling-oriented" people. "Thinkers" may be less aware of their level of anger and may be less willing to let others see their anger. "Thinkers" find anger a confusing emotion. When "thinkers" show their anger, they may do so without under-standing the effect that their emotional outburst has on others.

"Feeling" people evaluate problems and situations more emotionally and are therefore more likely to say things such as, "I don't like how that feels," or, "I feel good about this." They seem to be more in touch with their anger and able to express their angry feelings openly and freely.

When the extremes of these two types experience a situation in which they have been deprived of something desired, "thinkers" are more focussed on defining the problem and what can be done about it. "Feelers" are more focussed on their internal, emotional reactions to the problem rather than describing and solving it.

It is important to note that most people have a blend of thinking and feeling tendencies rather than pure emotional or thinking patterns. Knowing that people are oriented along these dimensions can help give you insight into your own anger and the anger of those around you. Where would you place yourself on this dimension? Also, as you read this booklet, you might find some sections easier to understand because of your thinking vs. feeling orientation.

Low vs. High Threshold for Anger

As we have seen, some people have a low threshold for anger. Individuals with a low threshold seem to be walking around with a chip on their shoulder just looking for an excuse to say, "Here, go ahead, knock it off." As soon as someone tries, they feel totally justified in "retaliating" and doing so with little remorse. The pain of grief in these individuals can amplify their preexisting tendencies toward anger.

By contrast, people with a high threshold for anger may still not show any visible anger reactions, even following the tragic death of someone they love. Or, they may feel an intensity of anger that they have never experienced before. For example, a 16 year-old boy whose 14 year-old sister was murdered by a school mate stated, "I never used to really get bugged by things. But now everything gets to me."

Short- vs. Long-Burners

When Short-Burners become angry, they return quickly to their pre-emotional level as demonstrated by a return of their body language, voice tone, and demeanor to their original state. When asked about their anger, these individuals report that they get over their anger quickly, sometimes almost instantaneously. By contrast, Long-Burners report that they continue to feel anger at nearly the same level of intensity for several minutes or hours after they erupt. These individuals often report that it is not until the next day—when they have had time to sleep on it—that they have returned to their pre-anger state. A few Long-Burners experience residual anger arousal for several days. There is little research on the effect of bereavement on a person's preexisting anger style.

Emotion Discriminators vs. Emotion Generalizers

Emotion Discriminators are exceptionally adept at sorting their emotional reactions and discerning subtle differences between feelings. They are able to distinguish between several different emotions they are experiencing at the moment.

By contrast, Emotion Generalizers find it difficult to identify what they are feeling even with a list of emotions in front of them. These individuals have been accused of "not trying hard enough" to share their inner world with those around them. When they get angry they report, "I'm mad", whereas the Discriminators might say, "I'm mad, but I'm also disappointed, agitated, hurt, and disgusted."

Confronters vs. Avoiders

One of the reasons people avoid angry encounters is because confrontation is simply too painful and anxiety-producing. According to John Gottman's research on couples [8], when some people are confronted in a conversation with information they consider too highly arousing (i.e., painful), they actually experience so much pain that they withdraw into themselves or get up and leave. The added importance of this finding for married couples is that the person who is most likely to leave is the husband. This suggests that discussing painful events, such as the death of a loved, one may actually be so painful for many men (and for some women), that they may literally have to leave the scene. More research is needed to understand these findings in terms of bereavement style. What researchers do know is that avoiding angry encounters is self-rewarding for Avoiders. That is, each time they avoid an angry encounter, they feel a reduction of anxiety which, itself, is a type of reward, and increases the probability that they will continue to avoid future angry encounters. Are you, or someone you live with, likely to leave during a discussion? Using a gentle and nonconfrontive approach, can you speak with this person?

A bereaved person who is more of a confronter would have little trouble expressing anger when it appears someone has crossed them. Have you been avoiding anyone in your life because of anger? Who do you think has been avoiding you because of your anger?

Introverts vs. Extraverts

When you become emotionally drained and need to "recharge your batteries," are you more likely to yearn for some quiet time? If so, you probably are more of an introvert. However, if you feel more energized after being involved in a group activity, then you're probably more of an extravert. When a death occurs in our life, our tendencies toward introversion or extraversion can certainly change.

Introverts are less inclined to initiate social interactions and are often described by others as withdrawn, cautious, and emotionally disengaged. Because they are so easily stressed by spontaneous social interactions and emotional confrontations, they may be more likely to express their anger in passive ways, such as pouting or giving others the "silent treatment." Extraverts are much more "people-oriented" and they tend be more impatient. Extraverts are more likely to show sudden, aggressive expressions of anger toward others. Which is more descriptive of you?

Self-Punishers vs. Other-Punishers

When angered, Self-Punishers have the tendency to turn their anger on themselves, even when someone else is clearly the cause of their anger. For self-punishers, the death of a child, spouse, partner, sibling, or parent, can increase the likelihood of self-punishing behavior such as: not attending social functions, eating too much or too little, neglecting one's health, hitting or cutting oneself, or suicidal behavior. As a way to cope with their anger during bereavement, Other-Punishers turn their anger on others, even when their own behavior provoked their anger.

21

High Need for Control

When a death occurs, people who have a high need for control in their life may be particularly devastated. The death of a relative or close friend can bring the life-shattering realization that much of life is beyond personal control. Bereaved people who are traumatized by this new realization typically make comments such as:

"Now I realize that anything can happen in my life."

"I was mistaken when I thought my life was something I could control."

"I now feel so out of control."

"I have no control over how the rest of my family grieves."

Thoughts such as these can be devastating for individuals with a high need for control and in some cases can lead to feelings of frustration and anger.

Components of Anger Expression

One way to think of anger is in terms of the way it affects our body, mind, social life, and emotional state.

The Physical Component

1. **Verbal expressions**
   - Swear words
   - Substitute swear words: "shoot, dang, darn, heck, son of a gun, cripes"
   - Labeling words: "idiot, stupid, heartless, psycho, chicken, geek, nerd"
   - Questions: "why. . ., who . . . , what . . . , when . . . , where . . . , how . . . "
   - Commands: "You shouldn't. . ., should've. . ., must. . ., need to. . ."

2. **Voice Tone and Intensity**

   Anger is easily noticed in an angry person's tone of voice. The better you know someone, the more adept you are at picking up even subtle cues in the voice tone. Sometimes you will get two messages from a person. When a person yells, "I'm not angry!" it's more likely you'll believe the message from the tone of voice than the message in the words. Voice intensity occurs simultaneously with voice tone. Some people's voices get quieter as they become angrier, while others become louder. How do you sound when you are angry?

3. **Silence**

   One of the most powerful means of showing anger is silence. It comes in a variety of forms: the silent stare, silence following a question, and the silent treatment.

4. **Body Language**

   People tend to stiffen their bodies when they are angry, particularly the muscles in the neck. Anger frequently triggers facial changes, such as: contortions, redness, dilated pupils, squinted eyes, curled lower lip, forward-jutted jaw, or clenched teeth.

Some of the most common hand motions that express anger are: fist shaking, finger thrusting (pointing toward another), karate chopping (a vertical downward slice with an open palm), fist of one hand hitting the palm of your other hand, open palm(s) facing toward another person, (indicating "get out of here!"), and the middle finger thrusting upwards toward another person.

5. Aggressive Behaviors

Examples of aggressive behaviors include: invading another individual's personal space, yelling, screaming, grabbing, pinching, pushing, punching, pounding, hitting, slapping, slugging, scratching, biting and kicking.

The Cognitive Component

The cognitive component refers to what you are thinking or perceiving at the time you are angry. Two examples of the cognitive component are Self-Talk and Anger Schema.

1. Self-Talk

Consider the anger you have been feeling since the death of your loved one. What do you say to yourself when you are angry? The self-talk of grieving individuals may include:
"I'm so angry about this."
"They can't do this to me."
"Why did this happen?"
"I hate living."
"I'm not going to take this!"
"This is the last straw!"

2. Anger Schema

A schema is a set of related ideas stored in our brain. For example, we have a cluster of related concepts about the way that men and women in our society should look and act. This is called our Gender Schema. If you saw a person with a beard and were told that person was a woman, your Gender Schema wouldn't have a place to put such information.

What does schema have to do with anger during bereavement? When a loved one dies, an Anger Schema may be activated whenever a bereaved person encounters anything related to the death. For example, people whose loved one was murdered report becoming very angry at things which did not elicit their anger prior to their loved one's murder. Now their Anger Schema is activated whenever they encounter such things as: violence in the media, unjust treatment of one person by another, ineptness in the justice system, and media glorification of a violent news story. What activates your anger?

The Social Component

While it is true that people get mad at themselves, it is more common for anger to be directed at other people. How would you answer the following questions related to your life now?

Who have I pushed away with my anger?

Who has pushed me away?

Who has not been there to give me the support I expected?

What have people said (and not said) about my loved one or my bereavement that has made me angry?

The Emotional Component

What we sometimes call "anger," could be another feeling such as animosity, annoyance, bitterness, disgust, displeasure, exasperation, indignation, irritation, or resentment. See pages 39 and 40 for a more complete list. Telling someone they don't have a right to be angry is the same thing as saying they do not have a right to experience their own emotions. As we stated on page 1, it is okay to feel angry, but not all forms of anger expression are helpful. The challenge with anger is choosing what you will *do* with it. Focusing on how you express and manage your anger is the key to using your anger constructively. Let's look at this further.

THE BEST ACTION PLAN FOR ANGER

Does screaming, hitting and/or kicking an object or throwing and breaking things help rid you of your anger? Is a physical display of anger cathartic, or does it reinforce (and eventually escalate into) more anger? The term "catharsis" refers to "emotional cleansing." According to this theory, doing something physical, such as screaming, hitting, or just talking angrily is supposed to cleanse people of their angry feelings.

Advocates for "catharsis" may see a grieving person's problem with anger as medically analogous to an "infected wound" that needs cleansing, rather than bandaging. They believe that healing can only come when the "wound" is reopened and cleaned out. When applying this theory to a person's anger, they conclude that encouraging the patient to "let it all out" is the best way to resolve or decrease anger.

After more than 20 years of research on this question it appears that, for the majority of people, screaming or hitting even "safe objects" (such as punching bags or pillows), does not "clean out the wound of anger." The findings of the studies have revealed that such behavior simply trains people to associate hitting or screaming with anger. Because hitting and screaming can feel good momentarily, these behaviors eventually develop into an automatic response to anger. Not only are cathartic behaviors hurtful when used on people rather than "safe objects," research has proven these behaviors **ineffective** for reducing anger. Instead, it may be much more helpful to talk with a close friend or a professional who is able to help you discover the real source of your deep-seated anger or how to let go of old hurts without conditioning yourself to become more physical when you are angry. Let's look at the next section to explore targets of anger.

Targets of Anger

When people become angry following (or, in some cases, prior to) the death of a loved one, there are a number of possible "targets" for their anger. Here are some common ones.

Non-Supportive People

Many bereaved people report that they are angry at the lack of support they had hoped for and expected from friends and relatives. In some cases the friends and relatives leave and never return. Widowed people report feeling like a "fifth wheel" with many of their married friends. Many bereaved people find that, years after the death, the friends who used to be in their address book have changed. Feelings of abandonment and isolation, compounding the person's grief, can result in both disappointment and anger. Has this happened to you? How has this affected you?

People Who Want You to Be Over It

Sometimes people who do remain involved with the bereaved person eventually indicate "it is time to move on." Their message may be sent directly or in more subtle forms. Examples of how this ill- received message is sent include:
"It's been long enough."
"I want your old self back."
"Life goes on."
"I hope you are putting this thing behind you."
For many bereaved people these statements bring out angry feelings. It seems clear to the bereaved person that those who offer this "advice" don't understand what it means to lose someone important to them. Or, if they do, they certainly don't seem to understand what it means to the person they're "advising." Often, people watching someone cope with the gut-wrenching journey of grief wish the bereaved person were over it. This is due in part to the difficulty they face, watching the unremitting pain of grief in someone they love. When they resort to using words that say

"Stop being in grief," it probably means, "I can't handle watching this continue." Your anger may also be provoked when people, who see you having a good time laughing or joking, begin to believe that it didn't take you long to "get over" your grief.

People Who Give the Wrong Type of Support or Who Grieve "Incorrectly"

Well-meaning people sometimes say things to newly bereaved friends and loved ones that indicate "they just don't get it." Such nonsupportive comments and cliches are also a source of anger. See if you recognize some of these inept classics:

"It's better this way."
"It's for the best."
"You'll get over (or make it through) this."
"It was God's will."
"I know just how you feel."
"She's in a better place now."
"If you need anything, just call me."

Anger can emerge during bereavement when two people grieving the same person's death have different expectations of the "right" way to grieve. Frustrations sometimes arise not only about our own perceived inability to grieve "correctly," but also because we may be upset at others who cry too little or too much, have too little or too much anger, or talk too little or too much about the deceased. Do you see yourself in any of these examples?

People Who Act Like Nothing Has Happened

Another potential anger target are those people who, after they've "paid their respects" at the funeral, act as if the death never occurred. They avoid you in the grocery store. Or, when they do approach you, they never ask how you're doing. These people ignore your grief reactions; or if they can't be ignored, they quickly try to change the subject. If there is anyone who has behaved this way with you, how are you coping with it?

People Who Don't Talk About Your Loved One

Perhaps even more frustrating for you, are people who act as if the loved one you are grieving for never existed. Like the people who act like nothing has happened, they may realize that, if you can lose a loved one, so can they. Never do you hear from them what you yearn to hear: the name of your loved one and the stories and memories that are so precious to you. See page 51 for a few suggestions to encourage others to talk about your loved one.

People Who Don't Realize What They Have

When you are grieving, you have a heartfelt understanding that life can be taken away in an instant. So, when people around you seem to be taking life for granted, it is not surprising that their behavior provokes your anger. Bereaved parents report the frustration of watching a mother or father in the supermarket yell or scream at or hit a child. The bereaved parent may feel like grabbing the offending parent and saying, "Stop it. You should be thankful that you have a child. Mine died!" While few parents have ever done this, most have been tempted to do so.

People Who Distort the Story of the Person's Life and Death

Anger can be easily evoked by ill-informed and seemingly uncaring people who generate inaccurate, false, or misleading stories about the life and death of the person you are mourning. Sadly, inaccuracies about events surrounding deaths from suicides, homicides, accidents, and unknown causes are far too common. This is especially true when the media become involved. Reports of death on television, radio, the internet, and in the newspaper have added to the anger and grief of bereaved friends and relatives. (See page 48 for dealing with the media.)

Chronic illnesses are also not safe from rumor or innuendo. If a person died from pneumonia or another opportunistic infection, the whisper of AIDS may float around the community. If the person died from AIDS, then stories of the origin of infection may circulate.

People Who Provide Scapegoating Targets for You

In the section on Defense Mechanisms we discussed how displaced anger is shifted away from the original target. Even under normal circumstances, life provides many opportunities for irritation and anger. For instance, you may get upset with drivers who tailgate or cut in front of you, people who shirk their responsibility, rude salespersons, people who crowd ahead of you in line, or someone who lied to you. But, when you are grieving the death of your loved one, these irritating challenges may seem even more annoying. As you struggle with the anger you feel about your loved one's death, you may feel tempted to wish that someone would tick you off, so that you would have a "legitimate" excuse to let your anger fly. Of course, if you do act out your anger in this way, the person to whom you are directing your tirade may either wonder why you're acting like a maniac, or they might even be a volatile person who quickly begins to retaliate, resulting in you suffering serious injury.

People Who Are Directly Responsible

If there is a person whose behavior or negligence led to the death of your loved one, you have a significant challenge, especially when it comes to your anger. One source of anger is the failure of the person responsible for the death to say, "I did this." or "I'm sorry." We are not going to tell you that you must forgive. Some family and friends of people who have died by the actions of another do forgive, while others do not. You can use this booklet to help you look deeply into your anger. After doing so, it is still your decision what to do with your anger. If you are considering doing something drastic, consider what effect your actions would have on the other people in your life—children, siblings, parents, friends. What effect would your revengeful actions have on their lives during the following year? Five years? Ten years?

People Who Are Indirectly Responsible

Are there people who could have done more in preventing the death? Who are they? Was there someone who knew something or was there a person who failed to be a good samaritan? Do other people agree with you or are you alone in your belief? Have they taken any responsibility for their actions? Maybe there is someone you can speak with about this. If you decide to do something drastic, it is again important to consider what effect your anger reactions would have on the significant people in your life.

People Associated With the Death

As you know, when death occurs, there are many people you may encounter: medical staff, police, clergy, counselors, psychologists, psychiatrists, funeral home directors, media reporters, medical examiners, or coroners. Despite the fact that these people may have had no hand in causing the death, you may still feel that their behavior added to your pain.

God

It's OK to be angry at God. For some bereaved people the harsh fact of death challenges them to question their conception of God. They ask, "How could God do this to me?" In his book, When Bad Things Happen to Good People, Rabbi Harold Kushner [9] asked that question countless times as he watched his young son slowly die of the aging disease called progeria. He could not understand why God, to whom Kushner had dedicated his life, would be so cruel as to take his son away. After much thought and discussion with others who had suffered great loss, he had to conclude that God did not *do* this to him. God doesn't sit in heaven directing events that bring joy, pain, or tragedy to our lives. Kushner concluded that it was not God who killed his son. But, it was God who was behind the hundreds of caring acts bestowed on his family by wonderful, kind human beings.

Not all people agree with Kushner's ideas. Some people do not believe in God; or they once did, but lost their faith. If you have such issues that you feel ready to address, ask yourself, "Is there anything I can do about this?" "Who could I speak with about this?"

Anger at Oneself

Following a death, a common target for anger is oneself. See if any of the following types of self-directed anger relate to you:

Self-hatred. If you feel any responsibility for your loved one's death, you may have made some of the following statements to yourself: "I'm a bad person." " I hate myself." "How could I have done that (or failed to do it)?" "Everyone would be better off if I were dead."

Neglect of health. People who hate themselves may say things such as: "Why do anything for myself? I don't deserve it." "Why go to the doctor? If I become (more) ill, so what? I deserve it." "If I don't feel like eating, why force it? I'm not worth it." This may be one of the reasons that bereaved people tend to have more health problems. Sometimes they feel that they do not have a "right" to take care of themselves. As a result of their lack of preventive self-care, they develop health problems.

Self-Punishment. Stemming from self-hatred, self-punishment behaviors include such physical actions on oneself as: hitting, slapping, cutting, biting, scratching, and butting one's head. If you are engaging in any of these behaviors, please find a way to stop. If you cannot stop yourself, it is important that you find a counselor to help you.

Deprivation of pleasure. Self-hatred can also take the form of depriving oneself of engaging in activities that formerly resulted in feelings of pleasure. Examples include depriving oneself of going out with friends, attending a movie, going to a sports event or dinner, laughing, engaging in sexual relations, participating in recreational activities, or taking a vacation.

Risk-taking. Some people react to a loved one's death by feeling that life isn't worth living. They begin to take risks that they wouldn't ordinarily take. Their self-talk may go something like this: "So what if I die or get hurt—it doesn't really matter." Examples of risk-taking are: reckless driving, experimenting with addictive drugs, unprotected sex with multiple partners, and trying dangerous activities without guidance (e.g., mountain climbing or hang-gliding).

Not living up to your own expectations. Part of being human is having expectations of yourself. Translated into self-talk, it often includes the words "should," "must," "have to," and "need to." During bereavement, it can sound like this: "I must be strong; I must do this right; I shouldn't feel this way; I need to work harder; or I have to accomplish this goal."

Sometimes the expectation comes from other people, including the person who died. A man in his mid-seventies, attending a lecture on loss, raised his hand and shared his experience. When he was a young man, his father died. As the oldest son, he was expected to take over the family responsibilities. It was only then, at this lecture, with tears in his eyes, that he clearly realized he had put his grief aside because he was expected to. When asked how long it had been, he replied in surprise, "My God, it's been 50 years!"

Expectations of others can, as with this man, lead us to put our grief work aside or make us feel guilty or angry at ourselves because we are unable to do so. Ask yourself the question: "What expectations do I have of myself, or do others have of me, that have caused me to be angry at or disappointed in myself?"

The Person Who Died

One of the most common targets of anger among bereaved people is the deceased person. This can be a difficult issue for the bereaved survivor because the target of one's anger is someone they cared for, who cannot defend themselves, and may have had no hand in their own demise. Some of the reasons anger is directed at the deceased person include:

Leaving. When people go out of our lives, we say that they "left." Some bereaved people report feeling anger that their loved one has left them, even when the death was not purposeful. Death by suicide often greatly intensifies the anger felt by those left behind. Do you feel some anger at your loved one for leaving you, even though you know it wasn't purposely directed at you?

The pain the death has caused. You may be experiencing some of the most intense emotional pain of your life. Some of the reasons may be: the finality of death—realizing that you will never see your loved one alive again, the manner of the death, other events surrounding the death, the hardships this death has created for you, the hardships it has bestowed on your family, and the loneliness and emptiness you feel. Anger may creep in when this deep pain persists.

Past transgressions. You may still have anger over things that the deceased person said or did to you or to other people. This can be particularly frustrating when the person dies before critical issues are resolved.

Not trying hard enough to live. Anger can enter into bereavement if you feel that the person who died could have "tried harder" to overcome the eventual cause of death. You are vulnerable to anger when you believe the person could have won the battle against death if she or he really loved you.

Negligence. Did the person fail to do something that may have led to the death? This is a blunt question. Answering it may put you more in touch with feelings of anger or disappointment. For example, if the person died because of alcohol or drug addiction, a smoking-related illness, or from a chronic illness or heart attack, you may be angry or disappointed that the person didn't get help sooner. Or, if the death were sudden, you may question whether the person could have done anything to prevent it.

Actions that led to the death. When death is by suicide, the survivors have a significant challenge in dealing with their anger at the deceased. The intentional taking of one's own life leaves those who knew this person with unanswered questions, unfinished business, and unfulfilled lives. Any or all of these can be a source of anger at the person who died.

Sometimes the person engaged in high risk behavior that led to unintentional death: reckless driving, use of drugs and/ or alcohol, unsafe use of firearms, illegal activities, or fighting. Anger may be directed at the deceased person for not acting more responsibly.

Jealousy of favored status. "The dead can do no wrong," is one of the beliefs that make it difficult to feel anger at a deceased person. However, the saintly status into which deceased people are sometimes placed can be cause for some of the survivors— notably siblings whose brother or sister died—to resent the person. When death follows a lengthy illness, the ill person may have been the focus of the household. The neglect that the survivors felt may have turned to anger against the dying/ deceased person. Feelings of resentment toward a deceased person may be difficult to admit. If you are experiencing such feelings, remember, they are normal.

Life in General

Newly bereaved people often report being ticked off at the world. Other people's happiness can easily trigger their anger. If they see people having a good time, laughing, their reaction is, "Sure, they can live it up. Their life hasn't been devastated." Some bereaved people report that the death has left them "floating" with no purpose, and that they feel jealous of--and angry at--the people around them who appear to be living a happy life. On the other hand, if they see people sad, angry, or lethargic, they feel indignant. They question, "What have they got to be upset about? They don't know what real problems are!" Bereaved people often describe the world as cold, gray, and lifeless. Some doubt they will ever be able to experience real joy, and some are certain no one can match their degree of sorrow.

INTENTIONS OF ANGER

This section provides an opportunity for you to think back on the anger you have been feeling and ask the question, "When I get angry, what do I want to accomplish with my anger?" See which of the following actions might describe your intentions.

To be hurtful to others and/or myself because I am hurting

When you are hurting from your anger, you have three choices: hurt others, hurt yourself, or hurt no one. Typically, when people hurt those they care about by the way they express their anger, the end result is frustration with themselves for the pain they caused. Who have you hurt with your anger? If you want to explore ways to stop doing this, read on.

To communicate

As mentioned earlier, anger is a way to let other people know that you are reacting to being deprived of something valued. There are times you may want others to be aware of your anger, times that you don't want them to know, and other times you may not have the energy to care one way or the other.

To release pent-up emotions

When you "let out" your anger, you may also be releasing other emotions. More important than your decision to let out your emotions, is your choice of *how* you let them out.

Unknown

Sometimes people may not care what their anger is "intended" to do. Perhaps they are thinking, "I'm upset and I don't care about intentions or anything else." When people are consumed by the pain of their grieving, they may be oblivious to their intentions. The more emotionally intense you allow yourself to become, the more difficult it is to get in touch with your intentions.

It's easier to be angry than sad

A few weeks after the death of his father, a man said, "You know, it's easier to be angry than it is to be sad. I hate being sad." For some people, anger is a much more "familiar" or comfortable way to react to grief than sorrow. On the other hand, especially during the early period of bereavement, some people are so overcome with sorrow or other grief reactions that they have no room for anger.

Showing anger to gain recognition

Sometimes negative attention is better than no attention. When people feel alone with their grief, they may hunger for any indication that others recognize their presence. Getting negative attention for their anger may seem preferable to being ignored. Beginning on the next page are ways to handle your anger.

Suggestions for Coping with Anger

Reading this booklet demonstrates your resolve to work on your anger. This section contains a variety of healthy ways to express and cope with your anger. As you read, select a few of the suggestions that you believe would be most helpful for you. Then begin to put them into practice. Many of the following suggestions involve some writing. Most readers find it convenient to have some paper and a pen within their reach while reading through this section.

Identify reasons for working on your anger

You can increase your success for working on your anger if you have a clear understanding of *why* you feel motivated to succeed. Write a list, including the following five topics:

1) All of the reasons you desire to work on your anger
2) How you would feel if you were never able to get more control of your anger
3) All of the feelings you are presently feeling right this moment
4) All of the feelings you think you are trying to avoid
5) All the feelings you desire to experience once you learn to control your anger

Once you have completed your list, post it in a place where you will see it each day. Your list will serve as a powerful reminder to you of all of the benefits you will gain from working on your anger. If you haven't yet finished your list, don't be discouraged. You are to be applauded for your interest in learning more about anger in the bereavement process.

If you've had thoughts or are thinking about suicide

Following the death of a loved one, thoughts about taking one's own life are normal. Bereaved people may wrestle with life and death feelings such as, "If I kill myself or let myself die, this horrible emptiness and pain will stop and I'll be with my loved one again." Such thoughts can seduce you into taking risks that could lead to your death. Risk-taking could involve driving recklessly, rehearsing a suicidal method such as pointing a firearm at yourself, collecting pills, or getting a rope.

If you are thinking about--or are actually engaging in--*any* risk-taking, suicidal behavior, the pain of your grief is obviously excruciating. However, help is available for your pain. Treasure your life by seeking help. Counselors who know about the anguish of bereavement have been able to help many bereaved people survive. You don't have to be alone. Choose to live and continue your journey through the sometimes slow and painful process of bereavement. Think about how much pain you are in right now due to the death of your loved one. Next, if you have family and friends who also loved the person who died, think of the pain they're probably experiencing. Then try to imagine the additional pain your death would cause. Finally, what would your deceased loved one say to you right now?
Please live.

Identify reasons for your anger

Look at each of the words in the following chart. Circle all the words that complete the following phrase: "The last time I **really** got angry was because I felt _____ ." This exercise will help you identify your anger triggers:

Abandoned	Controlled	Humiliated	Rejected
Abused	Deceived	Ignored	Ridiculed
Betrayed	Dominated	Insulted	Sabotaged
Bothered	Exploited	Offended	Smothered
Bugged	Frustrated	Patronized	Used
Cheated	Harassed	Put off	Vexed

My comments on the words I have circled are:_____
_____
_____
_____
_____

Identify your anger-related feelings

Circle all the words that complete the following phrase: 'The last time I was angry at someone, I also felt_____."

Aggravated	Exasperated	Nauseated
Agitated	Frustrated	Outraged
Anguished	Furious	Perturbed
Annoyed	Hateful	Rageful
Antagonistic	Hostile	Rebellious
Belligerent	Hurt	Repulsed
Bitter	Impatient	Resentful
Boxed in	Incensed	Revengeful
Burned up	Indignant	Smothered
Cross	Intolerant	Ticked off
Disgusted	Irked	Uptight
Dismayed	Irritated	Vicious
Displeased	Mad	Vindictive
Distressed	Mean	Violent
Enraged	Miffed	Volatile

My comments on the words I have circled are: _____

_____

_____

_____

When I'm feeling angry I am aware that my body usually:

_____

_____

_____

Using the following list, identify the targets of your anger since the death of your loved one:

Abusive/violent people	Legal system
Clergy	Media violence
Counselors	Medical examiner or coroner
Criminal justice system	Medical staff, doctors, nurses
Criminals	Myself
Deceased loved one	People taking life for granted
Disease that took my loved one	Person(s) responsible for the death
Drunk drivers	Police
Friends and ex-friends	Politicians
Funeral home personnel	Psychiatrists/Psychologists
God	Radio & TV reporters
Government agencies	Relatives
Grief experts and authors	Sad people
Happy people	Teachers
Immediate family	The world in general
Insurance company	

Create "I" messages

One of the most effective ways to communicate your anger toward another person is by expressing your feelings with "I" *messages*. How might you respond to a friend who recently angered you with a critical remark? Let's say that you have a friend named Tina, who is lecturing you and screams, "You've just got to get a life for goodness sakes! You need to move on-- your sister died more than six months ago!"

You may be tempted to tell Tina to "Shut up!" Instead, take a couple deep breaths, relax your body, get in touch with your intentions, and think how you will respond assertively and nonhurtfully to Tina, or anyone else, who has hurt your feelings or angered you. Perhaps you feel unprepared to give an "I" *message*. The four basic steps are outlined for you on the next page.

Step 1. *State your feeling*

When you feel confident you can deliver your message in an emotionally neutral, calm, quiet, polite, yet firm tone of voice, state your feeling, "Tina, last Monday after our talk, I walked away feeling burned up." After an anger-triggering event, take as much time as you need (a few minutes, hours, or longer) to feel calm and in control of the tone of your voice prior to beginning your *"I" message*.

Step 2. *Describe the offensive behavior*

Continue your *"I" message* by calmly specifying what was upsetting to you, "I was really angry when I heard the words indicating I needed to 'move on' from my sister's death."

Step 3. *State the reason for your feeling*

Next, explain why the person's behavior was upsetting, "I was feeling pressure to use your time line for 'moving on.' I thought my feelings or needs weren't being understood."

Step 4. *Listen to the person's response without interruption*

Continuing with the same scenario, if Tina is able and willing to give what you feel is a sincere apology, then your *"I" message* may have been effective. Only time and Tina's future behavior will offer proof of the effectiveness of your message delivery. If Tina is willing to listen, this may be a good time to help her begin to learn what she can say to be supportive to you.

The *"I" message* is a direct and effective method of communicating anger in a nonhurtful and assertive manner. However, even the most effective use of *"I" messages* cannot control how the other person will respond. In other words, you may do an excellent job delivering your *"I" message* and still find that the recipient responds negatively to your message. Be patient in trying to deliver an *"I" message*. It sometimes takes quite a few attempts.

If Tina becomes defensive and angry, and refuses to listen to the content of your *"I" message*, honor and respect **her** refusal to listen to you--as difficult as this might be. At this point, you can refuse to argue with Tina. You may find it more productive in the long-run to suspend your attempt to increase her understanding of your feelings and focus instead on reducing the intensity of Tina's angry feelings. By doing this, you demonstrate respect for Tina. This process is often an effective way to increase the other person's willingness to listen to you. Your *"I" messages* will be most effective when the intended recipient is ready to listen out of respect for you.

Keys to managing anger

If you feel your anger toward someone is escalating, should you leave (and avoid confrontation), or stay (and express your feelings)? This is one of the most critical issues in coping with anger. In deciding to *fight* or take *flight*, it may be helpful to look over these five *Keys to Managing Anger*.

1. **Develop self-awareness using the** *Fishbowl Technique*
    As the illustration depicts, the fishbowl technique can help increase your self-awareness of every aspect of your response to an anger-provoking situation while it is occurring. Using your imagination, you can place yourself inside the fishbowl actively involved in an angry interaction with another person while simultaneously remaining outside the fishbowl observing the entire interaction as calmly and objectively as you would observe a goldfish in a bowl.

    In the following illustration pretend you are Tom. Picture yourself (Tom) interacting with Tina. Also picture yourself as Tom watching two people (Tom and Tina). Putting yourself and your interaction inside the Fishbowl helps you gain the perspective you need to deliver the optimal message.

SELF-AWARENES

2. **Understand and accept that anger is a natural emotion.**
   Anger is a physiological reaction that is usually experienced
   as an automatic response to other feelings such as hurt, fear,
   or frustration. The more willing you are to accept that anger
   itself is a human reaction and that expressions of anger are
   based on choices, the more you will be able to manage your
   anger and cope with the anger of people around you.

3. **Learn your personal patterns of anger.**
   Become aware of what triggers your anger and what causes
   the intensity of your anger to escalate into an expression of
   anger:
   • External Cues: See Targets listed on pages 27-35
   • Physical Cues: Refer to your survey answers on page 40
   • Mental Cues: What are you saying to yourself?
   • Emotional Cues: Refer to the feelings you circled on page 40

4. **Actions that you can take when you begin to feel angry:**
   • **Take in a *deep* breath, breathe normally, take in another
     deep breath.**
   • **Take a time out**—take yourself out of your environment.
     (Make sure you first inform the other person.)
   • **Thought stopping**–In order to get your mind off the anger
     trigger, it can be helpful to say in your mind the word
     "**STOP**!!" This can serve to disrupt the obsessive thinking
     that sometimes increases your feelings of anger.
   • **Relax**–Close your eyes, visualize yourself in a safe and
     tranquil place, then, using your inner voice, calmly say,
     "(your name), relax."
   • **Count** to yourself in a calm, soft, soothing, even rhythm.
   • **Make yourself aware of your intention** by asking "Is my
     present intention to be hurtful or nonhurtful?"
   • **Choose** how intense your anger will be, how long it will last,
     and what you will do with it. The death of a loved one can
     create roadblocks along your journey of life. You can
     choose to keep your focus on what you cannot control and
     allow those roadblocks to develop into seemingly
     insurmountable barriers; or you can focus on what you

can control: your internal power to find creative ways around some of the barriers. It's your choice.

- **Problem-solve** by asking yourself, "Why am I angry? What do I ultimately want from this anger-provoking situation?" and "How can I get what I want?"
- **Call for assistanc**e, by asking, "Who can help me with this so that I can avoid acting out my anger?"
- **Emotionally disengage.** Whenever you increase your emotional, mental, or sometimes even physical distance from a provocation, you will experience more control over the intensity of your emotional response. Emotionally disengaging is most effective when done prior to becoming involved in a situation. By reducing your emotional investment in a situation, the emotional impact will be significantly reduced. Emotionally disengaging helps put your emotions closer to neutral and react to the situation as if it were happening to a stranger.
- **Remind yourself that "this too shall pass."** This gentle reminder can help increase your emotional or mental distance from the person or situation provoking your anger. No matter how entrapped you feel by a particular situation, or how anger-provoking it appears, you are free to decide how much or how little it will impact your life. It is up to you to determine how emotionally entrenched you are.

5. **Long-term anger management strategies**
    - **Practice anger management** strategies well in advance of anger episodes.
    - **Adjust your expectations** of other people in your life. Ask yourself the question: "Can I expect less of certain people in my life?"
    - **Discuss your angry feeling**s with a trusted friend.
    - **Role play with a trusted friend** exactly how you would like to address a potential anger-triggering situation.
    - **Keep a daily journal**. As difficult as this may be for you at this time in your life, many bereaved people report that writing down their thoughts and feelings (or saying them into a tape recorder) is very helpful. Journaling appears to

help in two ways. First, by getting your feelings "out of your head," journaling helps you develop an under-standing of your feelings. Second, by reviewing your journal, you may gain a new perspective on your anger, your grief, and your life as you reflect on how you previously coped.

- **Keep an Anger Diary or Anger Awareness Log.** If you don't wish to keep a diary, but wish to focus on your anger, you can keep notes on a calendar of your anger-related issues.

Suggestions for taking time out

Identify the cues which signal your rising anger.

- Physiological changes: increased heart rate, rapid breathing, muscular contractions
- Awareness of your thoughts and self-talk such as:
   Labeling— "That lousy jerk!"
   Catastrophizing—"I can't stand this."
   Mind-reading— "He's doing that on purpose."
   Vengeance—"I'll get even with him"
- Specific anger behaviors, such as: fist-shaking, finger-pointing, jaw-clenching, yelling, or cursing

Establish the time-out habit.

Practice taking time out when you are barely frustrated. This helps you develop a habit of leaving an anger-provoking scene before your anger starts to escalate or becomes hurtful. Talk ahead of time with the people in your life to establish a *time out signal* that is neutral and nonblaming. Making a "T" signal with your hands or calmly stating "time out" usually works. Prior to ever using your time out signal, explain that the signal also symbolizes the respect you have for that person and the commitment you have to using your anger constructively.

Reducing conflict by implementing change

When you are in conflict with someone, you have three choices. Let's look at each:

Attempt to change the other person (so their behaviors more closely match your expectations).

Changing someone else is the strategy least likely to work. Bereaved people sometimes experience anger at the way people around them are grieving, or not grieving. For example, following the death of her husband a widowed woman observed that her adult children seemed to have, in her words, "Gone on with their lives." She wanted to change them by phoning them and yelling, "Wake up! Your father died! You still have a mother." Not only was she grieving the death of her husband, she was angry and disappointed that the death had not affected her children in the ways she had thought it should. As you might guess, begging, demanding, and threatening--while it certainly gave her children something to think about--all ultimately failed to lead to a permanent change in her children's behavior.

Change yourself (so your expectations more closely match their behaviors).

Have you ever been sure you understood someone and then gained more information which gave you a different perspective? Your anger may be fuelled by inaccurate information. The typical way we often make sense of another person's perplexing behavior is to fill in the information gaps with our own explanations. Not until you gain reliable information can you know how wrong (or right) your assumptions were. Talking with a trusted friend or grief counselor about your grief, your anger, and your theories about the other person's behavior can be a very helpful way to cope with your grief. Conversely, keeping your feelings and thoughts inside only serves to cement your anger and make you more convinced of the absolute rightness of your convictions. It takes a lot of work and courage to try and understand why people do the things they do, but it is often worth the effort.

Realize that their behaviors and your expectations don't match; then either become resolved to the differences or dissolve the relationship.

If you are unable to change the other person or your own perspectives, you can choose to ignore the controversial issues of your grief in one of two ways: not talk about certain difficult issues with the person involved; or not interact with that person anymore. Because anger can be such a divisive issue between people who might otherwise care for one another, sometimes they make a decision not to discuss certain topics. For example, a year after her brother was murdered, a woman found that her only surviving brother wanted to forgive the murderer, something that she said, "made me sick." After many arguments, some yelling, and many tears, they mutually decided to exclude any mention of forgiving their brother's murderer in their conversations with each other. By reaching this agreement, they could still talk about their grief and, more importantly, the memories of their beloved brother.

Had the woman and her brother not been able to agree on the scope of acceptable conversation topics, they may have come to the tragic point of severing their relationship. Has this happened in your life? If so, you may have also experienced other family members choosing sides or trying to maintain contact with both parties. Anger, resentment, pride, and unwillingness to compromise have kept family members apart to their death. Perhaps, in this list of suggestions, there is something you can do to rejoin a broken relationship or help prevent it from becoming severed. However, no one can control what choices other people will make.

Dealing with the media

An accident, suicide, homicide, or unknown cause of death typically becomes a news event. Much anger has been directed at the media for the way they sensationalize the events around the death and trivialize the pain of the loss. The first step in working with the media is to realize the majority of news reporters will not suddenly develop more compassion, respect, and responsibility for the privacy of bereaved families and friends. However, you can still take some control of the situation by choosing one reporter to be the exclusive contact person. If you call a reporter with this offer, you can use it as leverage to have more control over how the story gets reported. In addition, you can refer all other reporters to this one person by saying, "I give all my information to _____."

Dealing with the person directly (or indirectly) responsible for your loved one's death

If your loved one's death was partly or fully due to the actions or negligence of another person, we encourage you to consider the following suggestions:

Write the person. Consider writing a letter which you might not ever mail. This is a way to get in touch with all the feelings, thoughts, and reactions you have had and are presently experiencing toward this person. Hold nothing back. Since this can be a highly emotional experience, you may wish to do this at a time of day when you have no other engagements.

Caution: Do not mail this letter until several days or weeks have gone by and you have shown it to a person you respect, and can trust to give you honest and objective feedback. Discuss with your trusted friend why you are really sending the letter and what you wish to accomplish in terms of your short and long-term intentions and goals. Also, seek to determine if your letter might interfere with any related legal proceedings. If you put the letter on a computer, you can revise it if you later choose to send it. If you do send it, make a copy for yourself. After you have given yourself some time to think about and discuss the letter, you may decide that it is best *not* to mail it.

Talk with the person. Make a list of all the pro's and con's of talking with this person. Consider discussing your list with a trusted friend who will listen empathically, nonjudgmentally, and objectively. When legal issues prohibit you from face-to-face contact with the person responsible for your loved one's death, writing to the person may be your most satisfactory option. It is important to understand that you can choose whether or not to contact this person. This is something that only you can decide.

If you decide to try to contact the person by phone or in person, use the same precautions and similar guidelines suggested for writing to the person. Find a respected friend with whom you can discuss issues such as: What do I expect this person to say or do? What if my expectations of this person are not met and no remorse is shown and no accountability is forthcoming? If you do arrange a person-to-person meeting, take someone with you for support and protection. Make sure your complete safety is assured.

It is vitally important to remember that, even if you directly confront the person or write a letter and receive the response you desired, you may still have anger issues that continue to need more work. In other words, do not place all your hope on this method as the only or ultimate way to resolve your anger. If talking with or writing the person helps even a little, then you have moved forward.

Join a bereavement support group

Call your local crisis center or mental health organization to find a support group. Many communities have such groups for bereaved parents, siblings, and spouses. Some groups are designed for people who have experienced a specific loss, such as the death of a spouse. Other groups are open to anyone whose loved one has died. Bereavement support groups, which are typically lead by a trained facilitator, assist participants in discussing their life changes, and feelings of grief, including anger. Although such groups are not for every bereaved person, many people report that they didn't know how they would have made it without their support group.

Get professional help

If, after reading this booklet, you realize that your anger continues to disrupt your life-style, you may want to contact a professional (psychologist, psychiatrist, counselor, clergy) who *has training in understanding the bereavement process.* Make sure that you confirm this prior to making an appointment. Bereavement support groups sometimes maintain a list of preferred counselors. To visit a professional does not mean that you are "crazy." It means that you have decided to work on your life with the assistance of a trained professional. Some bereaved people find it helpful to attend a support group *and* get counseling while others find that their style of grief does not fit with these approaches.

Encourage friends and relatives to talk with you about the person

When people are asked, "Why don't you ever talk about the person who died?" most give the well-meaning answer, "I just don't want to cause them any more pain." This mistaken belief has silenced the stories that people like you are craving to hear. You may need to help others understand that you love to hear stories about your loved one, no matter how long ago the death occurred. Encourage family and friends to share full stories, not just generic descriptions such as, "He was a nice person," or "He had a good sense of humor." You may also need to explain that when they share their stories, you may respond by shedding some tears, but they will be positive tears of remembrance.

Ask yourself, "Who can I call or write to ask for a story about my loved one?" Then use the following topics that may help stimulate the memories: vacations, funniest moments, school events, shopping, hobbies, parties, church experiences, and talents.

CONCLUSION

Several times throughout this booklet we pointed out the fact that anger is a normal response to loss. We hope you have gained insight into anger in general and your own anger reactions in particular. Have patience with yourself as you cope with the death of a very important person in your life. At various times during the next few weeks and months refer back to sections of this booklet to help reinforce the techniques that are helpful. Periodically take a fresh look at the Anger Insight survey on pages 3 and 4 and the exercises on pages 39 and 40 to see if your anger responses have changed in a positive direction. If they haven't changed for the better, do you believe that your answers are within the normal range or do you feel that you might benefit from professional help? Hopefully you have come to realize that anger is a natural emotion, but what you *do* with your anger is up to you.

We wish you our best and, most importantly, peace of mind.

REFERENCES

[1]   Neufeldt, V. (1988). <u>Webster's new world dictionary</u>, NY: Webster's New World.

[2]   Rando, T.A. (Ed.) (1986). <u>Parental loss of a child</u>, Champaign, IL: Research Press Co., p. 15.

[3]   Hankins, G. & Hankins, C. (2000). <u>Prescription for anger: Coping with angry feelings and angry people</u>, Newberg, OR: Barclay Press, p. 6.

[4]   Ostrum, C. & Moriwaki, L. (1995, April 2) Anger: Living on the Edge. <u>The Seattle Times</u> Reprints.

[5]   Warren, N.C. (1990). <u>Make anger your ally: Harnessing one of your most powerful emotions</u>. Brentwood, TN: Wolgemuth and Hyatt.

[6]   Yochelson, S. & Samenow, S.E. (1976). <u>The criminal personality, Volume I: A profile for change</u>, NY: Jason Aronson.

[7]   Linn, E. (1986). <u>I know just how you feel. . . . Avoiding the cliches of grief</u>, Incline Village, NV: The Publishers Mark.

[8]   Gottman, J. (1994). <u>Why marriages succeed or fail. . . and how you can make yours last</u>, NY: Simon & Schuster.

[9]   Kushner, H.S. (1981). <u>When bad things happen to good people</u>, NY: Schocken Books.

ABOUT THE AUTHORS

Bob Baugher is a Psychology Instructor at Highline Community College near Seattle where he teaches courses in Death Education, Human Sexuality, Human Relations, and AIDS. As a certified death educator, counselor, and suicide intervention trainer, he has worked with bereaved parents, siblings, spouses, and children who have lost parents. Since 1987, Bob has served on the advisory board for the King County Chapter of The Compassionate Friends. As a clinician he has co-facilitated children's grief support groups and has also worked on a three-year research project with the University of Washington entitled *The Parent Bereavement Project*. He has written three other books:

- A Guide to Understanding Guilt During Bereavement
- A Guide for the Bereaved Survivor *with Marc Calija*
- Death Turns Allie's Family Upside Down *with Linda Wong Garl and Kris Baugher*
- Coping with a Death by Homicide *with Lew Cox*

Bob and his wife, Kris, have been married since 1969, and have two children, Janée and Shawn. They reside near Seattle.

Carol Hankins earned a B.A. in sociology, M.S. in Education, and a Graduate Certificate in Gerontology from Portland State University. Her career has focused on helping the elderly and their loved ones cope with the physical, cognitive, and emotional losses associated with aging and illnesses such as Alzheimer's. She has had extensive experience as a medical social worker. For the past eight years she has been the director of an adult day services program.

Gary Hankins received his Ph.D. in Counseling Psychology from Georgia State University. He is a nationally known consultant to and seminar leader in the areas of anger, stress, and communication for businesses, schools, law enforcement agencies, mental health agencies and institutions. He was on the psychology staff at Oregon State Hospital for 13 years. He has also been an educator for over 30 years, and is currently an adjunct professor for several Oregon colleges and universities. Gary teaches courses in psychology and the theory and practice of counseling and ethics, as well as offering courses in managing anger and stress on both the undergraduate and graduate levels. In addition, he is a popular, often requested guest on television and radio talk shows across the country.

Gary and Carol have coauthored three editions of their book <u>Prescription for Anger: Coping with Angry Feelings and Angry People</u>: Newberg, Oregon: Barclay Press, 2000; New York: Warner Books, 1993; and Beaverton, Oregon: Princess Publishing, 1988.

Carol and Gary have been married since 1971. They have made their home just southwest of Portland in Newberg, Oregon. Carol and Gary are blessed with a wonderful daughter and son-in-law, Michelle and Alan Akins. Carol and Gary's favorite activity is enjoying their granddaughter, Brynn, born February 18, 1997.

Acknowledgments

We thank the following people for their valuable input in reading drafts of this booklet. Many of our readers used their own experiences of bereavement in helping address the critical issue of anger. We are sincerely grateful for their assistance:

James Ashby	Juan Kenigstein
Fred & Snookey Barlow	Ronald Klungness
Jane Bennett	Laura L'Eplattenier
Frederick Benson	Vicki Little
Kimberly & Bill Brennan	Grecia Luke
Brooklyn Chapter TCF	Roberta Luther
Mary Lynne Carson	Pat Malone
Glen Cummins	Patricia Martin
Frank & Donna Dahm	Tom Mattson
Elaine Eggebraaten	Carolyn McKee
Marilyn Evans	Scott Mena
Judith Friedman	Roberta & Philip Probolsky
Dr. Jacqueline Goffaux	Ann Sechrist
Anne Hallman	Joanna Snyder
Nena Hargett	Wendy Terry
Alberta Heagle	Ruth Vance
	Dolores Ware

Special thanks also go to Bob's wife, Kris, for her love and support, and for her many hours of computer & production work in preparing this booklet.

Discounts for Ordering Multiple Copies

2-10 copies:	5% Discount
11-24 copies:	10% Discount
25-49 copies:	20% Discount
50-99 copies:	30% Discount
100 or more:	35% Discount

Price: $8.00 (U.S. funds) per copy.
Add $2.00 for postage for a single copy.
U.S. orders of 2 or more copies receive free postage.

Shipping billed according to postal rates on Canadian and out of U.S. orders.

Please allow 2-4 weeks for delivery.

Washington State residents add 9.5% sales tax.

Send Check or Money Order to:

Robert Baugher, Ph.D.
7108 127th Pl. S.E.
Newcastle, WA 98056-1325

or e-mail your order and you will be billed

b_kbaugher@yahoo.com

Pricing, discounts, and taxes subject to change without notice.